GEARING UP FOR SPORTS

SOFTBALL GEAR

NOAH RICCARDI

PowerKiDS press

Published in 2027 by The Rosen Publishing Group, Inc.
2544 Clinton Street, Buffalo, NY 14224

First Edition

Book Design: Madison Thogmartin

Photo Credits: Cover, pp. 1, 15 Jon Osumi/Shutterstock.com; p. 5 Victoria Amoro/Shutterstock.com; pp. 7, 19 Aaron of L. A. Photography/Shutterstock.com; p. 9 Mandy K. Photography/Shutterstock.com; pp. 11, 13 JoeSAPhotos/Shutterstock.com; pp. 17, 21 Jan de Wild/Shutterstock.com.

Cataloging-in-Publication Data
Names: Riccardi, Noah.
Title: Softball gear / Noah Riccardi.
Description: Buffalo, New York : PowerKids Press, 2027. | Series: Gearing up for sports! | Includes glossary and index.
Identifiers: ISBN 9781499456769 (pbk.) | ISBN 9781499456776 (library bound) | ISBN 9781499456783 (ebook)
Subjects: LCSH: Softball--Juvenile literature. | Softball--Equipment and supplies--Juvenile literature.
Classification: LCC GV881.15 R533 2027 | DDC 796.3578--dc23

Manufactured in China

CPSIA Compliance Information: Batch #QS27PK. For Further Information contact Rosen Publishing, at 1-800-237-9932.

CONTENTS

The Ball

Softball players play with a ball. The ball is round and hard. It is usually yellow with red **stitching**. Softballs are 3.8 inches (9.7 cm) across. They bounce less than balls in other sports.

The Bat

Players try to hit the ball with a bat. They hold a thin part called the **handle**. The bat's **barrel** is wider. It is 2.25 inches (5.7 cm) thick.

The handle of the bat has a special kind of tape. This helps batters hold the bat. The handle also has a knob on the end. This stops the bat from slipping out of players' hands.

22

Batter's Protection

Pitches can hit batters. So, batters use gear to protect themselves. They wear helmets on their heads. Helmets sometimes have wire cages on the front. Some players also wear padding to protect their **shins** and elbows.

The Glove

When the batter hits the ball, fielders try to catch it. Each fielder wears a glove. The glove has webbing and a pocket to catch the ball. The glove is made of **leather**. This protects the player's hand from the hard ball.

Catcher's Gear

The catcher's job is to catch pitches. Pitches can be very fast. So, the catcher's glove has extra padding. This helps the catcher's hand not get hurt.

The ball may also hit the catcher's body. To prevent **injuries**, the catcher wears protective gear. They wear a padded shield on their chest to block the ball. They also wear leg guards. A helmet covers their face and head.

MIZUNO
MIZUNO
SAMURAI

Face Guard

Infielders can get hit by the ball. To protect their faces, some infielders wear masks. Softball masks are made with wire. The wire forms a cage in front of the player's face.

Cardinals

Cleats

Softball players wear shoes with spikes on the bottom. These shoes are called cleats. They help players run on grass and dirt without slipping. They also help players stay **stable** when throwing the ball.

GLOSSARY

barrel: The thickest part of the bat.

handle: The part of the bat that a player holds.

injuries: When a player gets hurt during a game.

leather: A material made from an animal's skin.

shins: The front of the lower parts of the legs.

stable: Firm and steady.

stitching: Thread woven into an object to hold it together.

FOR MORE INFORMATION

BOOKS

Flynn, Brendan. *Baseball and Softball*. Minneapolis, MN: Abdo Publishing, 2024.

Leed, Percy. *The Summer Olympic Games*. Minneapolis, MN: Lerner Publications, 2025.

WEBSITES

Britannica Kids: Softball
kids.britannica.com/kids/article/softball/400183
Learn more about softball.

Olympics: Baseball/Softball
olympics.com/en/sports/baseball-softball/
Learn more about bat-and-ball sports at the Olympic Games.

INDEX